I0108829

For Michael

Copyright © 1994 by Winter Robinson
ISBN 978-1-948929-51-6
All rights reserved. No part of this book may be used or reproduced in any manner
whatsoever without written permission except in the case of brief quotations
embodied in critical articles and reviews
For information address Crossroad Press at 141 Brayden Dr., Hertford, NC 27944
A Panta Rei Production  - Panta Rei is an imprint of Crossroad Press.
www.crossroadpress.com

Crossroad Press Trade Edition

# REMEMBERING

## A Gentle Reminder of Who You Are

### by Winter Robinson

PANTA REI

# To the Reader

We cannot claim ownership of our thoughts, whether they are highly creative or mundane. Everything has been thought before, or, in the least, is being thought in this moment. This is what I believe. There are no new thoughts in this book. Everything within its pages you have heard, read or thought before. You will recognize the teachings of Jesus, Buddha, Don Juan, *A Course in Miracles*, Donald Shimoda, Robert McCammon, John Lennon, and Jon Kabat-Zinn to name some of those who have remembered and written about it. These thoughts have been specifically selected because they repeat themselves throughout history.

Every effort has been made to acknowledge copyright holders and I apologize if any omissions have been made. Please notify the publisher.

## Acknowledgments

I wish to thank all of those who have helped me bring *Remembering* to life: my editors: Caroline Tilton, Jean Templeton, and Pat Pinegar; Cindy Drew for her expertise in graphics, color and printing. And a special acknowledgment to Jennifer Lee for helping it come to life.

Carlos Castaneda, Jon Kabat-Zinn, Pete Russell, Richard Bach, and to all who have helped me remember, thank you.

This book is yours and it is intended to be used.
Please write or draw in it as you please.

I don't believe that we learn anything, we just remember.

When we were children, the practice of magic was an
everyday occurrence.
We could turn the simplest object into the most fantastic,
mind-boggling toy that you ever saw.

I remember turning two tin cans into my own personal
telephone so I could call my best friend.
It didn't work, of course.
It didn't need to.

Clouds were our own personal divining tools. Within them we could see deep into other realms of reality ... animals, birds, people, and dragons.

Those days, before we were schooled in "How the World" was, were the days when we were most in touch with the way life *really* is.

I think we were born into this world with all of the knowledge and magic the Universe has to offer.

We came into life knowing the way things worked, knowing that all we had to do was focus our intent and imagine.

School was introduced to make us forget that knowledge, because if we didn't, then we would know more than the grown-ups.
They might lose control if we continued to know.

It could be that they were just sad because somewhere, deep inside themselves, they knew that they had forgotten things that were pretty important to the way things operated.

Some of us, for whatever reason, are remembering.

Maybe it's because we still have that telephone to the *Stars*, or maybe it's because we've allowed ourselves to become bored with life. We are being forced to remember who we are, where we came from and how everything is connected.

I don't know the reasons.
I simply know we are remembering.

And so, here is a reminder of what you already know.

It is not to be learned, but remembered.

These reminders aren't in any particular order because the part of you that is remembering will open this book exactly to the place you need to be, with what you are remembering.

First and foremost, you know infinitely more about the mystery and magic of the Universe than you might suspect. Your conscious mind tries to keep this from you because it doesn't fit comfortably with what it has been taught.

...And second, the belief system you are using is the one that is operating.

Your purpose is to *wake up*.

There is an order to the Universe.
We can see the order when we slow down and pay attention to the synchronicity of things.

*In all chaos there is a cosmos, in all disorder a secret order.*

Carl Jung

There is no place to go.
You are already there.

There is no such thing as coincidence.

What we call miracles are natural.
If ever a miracle has occurred,
anywhere or anytime, then the law still holds.
The laws haven't changed.

The prevailing force in the Universe is Intent,
which, according to Don Juan,
changes and reorders things
or keeps them as they are.

In order to intend,
it is important that you be still,
listen,
and focus your awareness.

In addition to our personal intent, there are lines of intention
which guide all human experience.
As we grow in sensitivity
to the messages of life,
these fields make themselves known.
You can't manipulate these fields of intent.
You have to let them unfold, gradually.

Look at the edge.
Always look at the edge
to see what is important,
to see the in-between.

Deer step in between.

*Sitting quietly, doing nothing,*
*Spring comes, and the grass grows by itself.*

from the *Zemin Kushu*

Spirit shows itself to everyone,
with the same intensity.
As to whether you see it or not
depends upon where you focus
your awareness.

You are unique;
there is no need to compare
what you do or who you are
with anyone else.


You are more
than your physical body.

Your mind
creates your reality.

You make life up
as you go along.

There are no limitations.
You have made up what you believe
to be your boundaries and limitations.
Argue for them, and they are yours.

*Use what talents you possess.*
*The woods would be very silent*
*if no birds sang*
*except those that were the best.*

Henry Van Dyke

All happiness and unhappiness
comes from our thoughts.

Moment after moment
you create your own path.

Being awake
means being here now.
Not in the future, not in the past.
Here, now.

It is only
in the present moment
that you can work
magic.

It is only
in the present moment
that you can
create and manifest.

Start where you are.

There is a very subtle energy
that pervades the Universe.
When you slow down,
you can feel it.

Money
is your life energy.

Remember
that being asleep
is not being fully present.

It is possible to be awake
during your dreamtime,
to fly to distant places,
see old friends,
and create your days.

You always travel at night...
you just don't always remember.

When you fly,
you go where you think.

*To fly as fast as thought,*
*to anywhere there is,*
*you must begin by knowing*
*that you have already arrived.*

Richard Bach
*Jonathan Livingston Seagull*

*The trick ...is that we are trying*
*to overcome our limitations*
*in order, patiently.*

*We don't tackle*
*flying through rock*
*until a little later in the program.*

Richard Bach
*Jonathan Livingston Seagull*

To solve any problem,
sleep on it.

Love
is accepting ourselves
and others
as we really are.

Learning to love ourselves,
to not beat ourselves up for being human,
is one of our primary reasons
for living.

*It is only with the heart
that one can see rightly;
what is essential
is invisible to the eye.*

Antoine de Saint-Exupery
*The Little Prince*

Be willing to be vulnerable.
To love, to trust and
to open yourself to emotional communication
means you are willing to run the risk
of being hurt.

You are not neutral
toward those
who are
a reflection of yourself.

You are not your thoughts.

You are not your self-image,
nor your label.
Not your education, position, social status.
These are meaningless attachments.

Your attachment
to your self- image is learned,
and can keep you from remembering
the way things work.

Your self-image is a paradigm.
It is not who you really are.

Guilt is optional.

There are those who ask questions
for themselves...
There are those who ask questions
only about others...
And there are those
who will ask the *real* question
during the last five minutes
of our time together,
when there is no time to reply.

If you find yourself
trying to convince someone
of your Truth,
you don't believe it yourself.

Those who believe,
have nothing to prove.

Truth doesn't have to be complicated.

There is no such thing
as a mistake or failure;
it's all learning.

All nature is aware.
It is we who are unaware.

The earth
is a Sentient Being.

*God, or Nature?*

Spinoza

Everything you see
contains a message for you.

If you are looking for an answer,
the answer is wherever you choose
to focus your awareness.

Growth comes from your search for *Truth*.
Problems occur
when you think you have found *It*.

When you think
you have found a New Truth,
it is really Old Recognition.

Within every religion
and every belief system,
there is a piece of the Truth.

You do not have to defend
Truth.

You are a conduit for Spirit.
You may not know it
if you allow the world
to keep you busy.

You may hear your inner voice
or that of an Angel,
but you think it's you,
your thoughts and feelings.

Sometimes Spirit
will make itself known
by heightening one of your senses.

Spirit only tells you what is.
You draw the conclusions.

You are learning
about Trust.

*I never came upon any of my ideas
through the process of rational thinking.*

Albert Einstein

To ask
what is right or wrong
about a situation,
means you're too late
for the intuitive response.

You seek to
*just know.*

This is it.
This is life.
There is nothing to wait for.

You have no assurance
that your life will continue
beyond this moment.

*Death is not our enemy,*
*nor our destroyer.*
*It is our only worthy opponent.*
*We are born to take that challenge.*

Don Juan

You
cannot die.

Remember,
there are Angels.

The veil
between this world
and the next
is very thin.

If you are alive,
you are not finished.

*The river delights to lift us free,*
*if only we dare to let go.*

*Our true work is*
*this voyage,*
*this adventure.*

Richard Bach
*Illusions*

Everyone
has a life to save
while on this earth.

Suspend your disbelief.

Remember
that your health
is your responsibility.

Your body is thought
in a form
which you can see.

Each thought you think
has a biochemical effect
in your physical body.

There is no separation
between your mind
and your body.

*The physician
is only the servant of nature,
not her master.*

*Therefore, it behooves medicine
to follow the will of nature.*

Paracelsus (16th century physician)

There is a connection
between every sentient
being on the planet.

You *know*
when someone else
is thinking about you.

Everything is subtle energy.
We use subtle energy sexually,
or for psychic awareness,
or for healing.
We use subtle energy to nurture our cooking.

It is all the same energy.

*As you simplify your life,*
*the laws of the universe will be simpler.*

Henry David Thoreau

You can simplify your life.
You don't have to
answer the telephone
or run one more errand.

Creativity
is born from *chaos*.

Time
is derived from thyme,
the herb
that expands and expands.

Take nothing
that is not offered.

You don't have
to please anyone else.

However, you are obligated
to be true to yourself.

*When you find yourself saying,
"They say that..."
your fear has taken over.*

Ken Roberts

Fear
is an opportunity
to discover what
you really believe.

Every moment
is a new beginning.

*There are no*
*ordinary moments.*

Dan Millman

Your consciousness
dwells through many lifetimes
and many unseen universes.

Within one lifetime
are many lifetimes.

There are worlds upon worlds,
before your very eyes.

Things
can't make you happy.

Delete your need
to understand.

Touch the world around you
gently, sparingly
and with tenderness.

With a focus of awareness
all information
is available to you.
You can know the past,
the present
and the future.

We have the answers;
it is the questions
that are difficult.

*Mindfulness must be engaged.*
*Once there is seeing,*
*there must be acting.*
*Otherwise, what is the use of seeing?*

Thich Nhat Hanh

Of what use
is your intuition
if you do not act upon it?

You cannot steer anything
unless it is moving.

If you never take a risk
you'll never know your potential.
And you'll always wonder
if you could have...

Happiness is possible
only in this present moment.

Seize the moment.

What is true
for one member of the species
is potentially true
for any member.

You are inwardly trapped
with a false set of beliefs
about how to live your life.

*Any path is only a path,*
*and there is no affront,*
*to oneself or others,*
*in dropping it*
*if that is what your heart tells you.*

*Look at every path closely and deliberately.*
*Try it as many times as you think necessary.*
*Then ask yourself, and yourself alone,*
*one question...*
*does this path have a heart?*

*If it does, the path is good;*
*if it doesn't, it is of no use.*

Carlos Castaneda
*The Teachings of Don Juan*

You can always change your mind.

*Even if you are on the right track,
you'll get run over
if you just sit there.*

Will Rogers

What would you do
if you could not fail?

*Everything comes and goes.*
*Just let it be.*

Joseph Goldstein

Everything changes.

*The contradiction so puzzling
to the ordinary way of thinking
comes from the fact
that we have to use language
to communicate our inner experience,
which in its very nature
transcends linguistics.*

D.T. Suzuki

You seek *to know,*
without the intervention
of language.

You can only *experience* the Spirit;
you cannot talk about it.

To talk separates you from what is.

The more you experience Spirit,
the more difficult it is to explain.
You cannot.

*He who knows*
*does not speak.*
*He who speaks*
*does not know.*

Lao Tsu

There is power
in silence.

Choices are dictated
by silent knowledge.

Reading
can be a way
of not engaging in life.

Television
is the shadow side
of humanity.

*Be Here Now.*

Ram Dass

*By promoting,*
*creating*
*or allowing*
*events into your mind,*
*your life unfolds.*

Susan D'Amore

Do only one thing
at a time,
mindfully.

There is no
either/or.

We cannot claim ownership
of our thoughts,
whether they are highly creative
or mundane.

Everything
has been thought before,
or in the least,
is being thought in this moment.

*I am certain of nothing*
*but the holiness of the heart's affection*
*and the truth of the imagination.*

John Keats

Your imagination
is real.

In order to see a Spirit
you must catch it
in your peripheral vision.

Look
and See.

Remember
that there are many realities.

The Universe
gives "pop quizzes."

Freedom
Is the only driving force.

If you wish to be free,
let go of your attachment
to boredom.

*Perception is the spin
that we put on Awareness.*

Wayne Essel

You don't raise your consciousness,
you increase your *awareness*.

*Play it like it lies.*

Shivas Irons

Help
is always available.

*There is only here and now,*
*only this unfolding moment,*
*and this is the closest we can come*
*to Knowing*
*the Presence.*

Rabbi David Cooper

The future
foreshadows itself.

Somewhere,
in infinity,
what you desire is taking place.

*Expectation*
is the unspoken shadow of *Intent.*

Consciously, or unconsciously,
you attract into your life
what you believe in most strongly
or imagine most vividly.

If you don't know what you want,
you will not recognize it
when it appears.

*You are never given a wish*
*without also being given*
*the power to make it true.*

*You may have to work for it, however.*

Richard Bach
*Illusions*

154

*Life is either one great adventure,*
*or nothing at all.*

Helen Keller

Doing comes
when we take action.

There are simple things which we can do
to help us remember who we are,
where we are from
and where we are going.
These exercises are not new;
in fact, they are as old as time itself.

*I'm going to take a breath
and let myself exist for a while.*

Jennifer Lee

Being mindful
is being here now,
in this moment, with
all of your awareness.

Breathe mindfully.

Choose an activity,
something you do every day on automatic.

Resolve that for one week
you will use this activity
to wake up your mindfulness
by giving it full attention each time you do it.
It could be brushing your teeth,
or drinking your coffee in the morning.

For today,
create voluntary simplicity.
Do less
in order to do, or be, more.

Put your "to do" list aside.
Just be.

Allow the ringing of the telephone
be a reminder to return
to the present moment.

Form a question in your mind.
Look to the nearest tree or pool of water
to find your answer.

Stop,
look
and listen.

Sit quietly
and watch birds fly and eat.
Select one and stay with it
as it flies, eats, and sings or calls.

Close your eyes
and imagine
you are watching yourself— you are the bird.

Stay fully in the present
as you observe
and become the bird.

Watch a hive of bees.


Swim.
Become the water you already are.


*Breathe.*

Who are you?

How do you experience yourself?

Where do you experience yourself?

Explore a cave.
Stop and listen.
Ask yourself, "Who am I?"


Sit by a river, or the ocean.
Follow your breath.
Imagine that you are the river, the ocean.

Get up with the dawn.
Sit with nature.


Find a place
where you can be
with the stars.

Listen to music with a headset.
Begin by following your breath,
allowing your body and mind to relax.
Follow one instrument throughout.
You might begin with the melody
and then move on
to listening to the background instruments.


Experiment
with different types of music
and notice how your body feels
with each piece.

Creative manifestation
takes energy and action.
Write your desires.
Read your list aloud three times
when you first wake up
and just prior to going to sleep.

Create room
for your manifestations.

There is magic in threes.

Create quiet time
in which you can imagine
(feel, sense and/or visualize)
what you are creating.
Focus your thoughts *only*
on what you are manifesting.
Sense in as great detail as possible.
Put yourself in the picture
and see it as already existing.

To instantly manifest,
there must be *no* thought
between the imagery
and the actual doing.
For example,
imagine the perfect golf swing,
then swing.

To tell yourself
that you are going to swing the perfect swing
will separate you
from that which you are creating.

The thought interferes.

Don't tell anyone
what you are manifesting.

Remember
the power of silence.

Suspend your disbelief.

Who are you?
Look in the mirror.
Is this you?

Close your eyes,
follow your breath
from the tip of your nose
down into your stomach.

After following your breath,
imagine there is a subtle energy
that moves through your body,
along with your breath.

Rub your hands together,
pretend that you are forming
a ball of this energy.
Keep your eyes closed.
Sense the energy.
Make the ball larger,
then smaller.

Place your hands near a tree,
a plant or a human
and continue to sense the energy.

Increase your awareness
of what actually is.
Feeling is knowing.

Hold your hands, fingertips upward,
in front of you.
Let your eyes lose their focus;
look at your fingertips.

Think of someone you don't like
or who makes you uncomfortable.
How does he/she
mirror something in you?

Focus all of your awareness
on the person you are with.
If your mind wanders,
bring it back to the present moment.

Notice the space between your fingers,
between the leaves of a tree,
between the clouds.

Who are you?
Look at your environment.
Is this you?

Walk through your home at night,
using only touch to guide you.


Crawl through your home at night,
using only touch and smell to guide you.

Touch and *feel* everything—
the glass you are holding,
your clothing, your hair.
Be fully in the present
as you explore this way of feeling.

Look at the in-between
of anything.

Ask yourself,
"How does this person *feel?*"
And then notice how this question
affects the feelings throughout
your own body.

Taste a slice of lemon.

Place a piece of chocolate
on your tongue.

Notice.

Experiment with closing your eyes
in various locations
and noticing what you smell—
trees, bread baking, city smog.
What memories arise from each smell?

Before going to bed tonight,
tell yourself, "I'm going to fall asleep,
but I will consciously know
what is taking place during my dreams."

To fly,
suspend your belief that
you are limited
by your physical body.

In reality,
you are suspended
across space and time.

Who are you?
Touch your face, your body.
Is this you?
Who are you?
Be still.
Listen.
Is this you?

Who are you?
Write in a journal.
Is this you?

Say,
"Thank you."

Play the piano
or any instrument available to you...
If you don't have an instrument,
tap out a rhythm on a table
or make a sound with your voice.

Take a walk.
Walk slowly,
fully aware of how your feet
touch the ground,
of what is around you.

Imagine a problem.

Write it on a 3 x 5 card.

Imagine solutions.
Write them down.

Try and solve the problem
with as many different solutions
as you can think of.

Give yourself a deadline
for when you need the answer.

Ask the Universe for help.

Forget it.

Prior to sleep,
formulate a question or problem
as clearly as possible.

Then sleep on it.

To worry will exhaust the problem and you.

Don Juan

Take a walk.

Walk lightly,
bringing the energy
from the sky through you
in order to nurture the earth.

Take a walk.
Walk slowly.
Feel every motion of your body
as you shift your weight.
Notice your breath.


Expand your awareness as you walk.
Listen to all the sounds around you.

Help is always available.
Whether you are looking for a lost object
or trying to reach a decision.

Create a quiet space
and ask for what you seek.
Remember to say, "Thank you."

Ask for help.

Whenever you ask for help,
it is immediately answered
the moment you ask.

Touch your own palm.
You are the one touching
and the one feeling the touch.

What are you not doing in your life
that you want to do?
Make a list.

Observe your sexual feelings
and thoughts as they arise.
Don't judge them.

Mindfully clean out a closet.
If you haven't used something,
don't keep it.

With clear intent,
bring no harm in thought, word or deed
to any living creature
for one day, two days, for one week.


For ever.

Ask yourself
why you were born.

Keep asking.

Today,
act on every thought of generosity
that arises.

Just do it.

Draw a picture.
Try not to judge
how you are drawing.

Follow through
on what you start.

Do something
that you have been wanting to do
for a long time,
but haven't
because you haven't had time.

Remember to make every act count
because you are only here
for a short while.

Practice silence three times a day
for at least five minutes.

For today,
do not speak about anyone else,
positively or negatively.

Today,
treat every person
as you would like to be treated.

If not me, then who?

If not now, then when?

This book is a belief system.
*It could change.*

Keep searching..

# About the Author

Before realizing that my search for "Truth" was really a quest for deeper spiritual meaning, I snugly settled into an educational system that valued analytical reasoning. I chose to spend my time, my energy, and my mind building a career in the mental health field. Starting as a therapist for the Addiction Research Foundation in Toronto, I returned to the US to teach college level psychology classes and direct a continuing education program for mental health workers. But in the early '80s my carefully designed world of psychology and mental health flipped upside down. Working as an analyst for the state attorney general, I had a precognitive experience that was so detailed and accurate that it changed the way I saw reality.

Lately I wear many hats: author, consultant, educator, therapist, medical intuitive, permaculturist, gardner, "realist" and futurist. (The role of a futurist isn't about making lots of accurate predictions, but more the act of stimulating creative thought about the future that, in turn, influences how we act today.) I strongly believe that we must think differently: co-operate with each other, share resources, and work together as we enter a time of diminishing resources.

The last few years I have made an attempt to understand why we have come to peak everything. (I think that I know "how" we got here, just not why.) Now I just try live with the fact that most of us don't see it.

So, these days, instead of writing (or talking) about intuition, complimentary medicine, and magic, I write about energy descent, four season harvesting, the need for community, the need to prepare, and all matter of other things that are earth related.

And I'm up to my ears in chickens and green-house greens, a rooster who thinks the sun comes up at 3 AM, and so many projects I can't begin to list them. The planet is still getting warmer, energy is still descending, and our economy is still tipping (big time).

The I Ching cautions us to not forcefully try to change things, rather we need to rely on the beneficial action of nature to correct things.

Perhaps that is all we can do, rely on nature.

Warmly,

Winter

Curious about other Crossroad Press books?
Stop by our site:
http://store.crossroadpress.com
We offer quality writing
in digital, audio, and print formats.

Enter the code FIRSTBOOK
to get 20% off your first order from our store!
Stop by today!

www.ingramcontent.com/pod-product-compliance
Lightning Source LLC
Chambersburg PA
CBHW061819040426
42447CB00012B/2724